Blasted
&
Phaedra's Love

Blasted

'Kane has an acute grasp of sexual politics and her dialogue is both sparse and stunning. They will call her mad, but then they said that about Strindberg.' *Mail on Sunday*

'A serious writer with a talent for flinty dialogue in the Edward Bond mode.' *Independent on Sunday*

Phaedra's Love

'The performance is a rapid and exhilarating ride packed with silences to remember and words to reflect on.' *Time Out*

'Her sulphurous dialogue is full of reeking toughness and she brings just the right laconic inflections and dark comic edge to her material.' *Evening Standard*

Sarah Kane was born in 1971. Her first play, *Blasted*, was produced at the Royal Court Theatre Upstairs in 1995. Her second play, *Phaedra's Love*, was produced at the Gate Theatre in 1996. Her short film, *Skin*, produced by British Screen/Channel Four, premiered in autumn 1995. She is currently under commission to the Royal Court, Royal Shakespeare Company, Sphinx Theatre Company and British Film Institute.

Sarah Kane

Blasted
&
Phaedra's Love

Methuen Drama

Methuen Modern Plays

First published in Great Britain in 1996
by Methuen Drama
an imprint of Reed International Books Ltd
Michelin House, 81 Fulham Road, London SW3 6RB
and Auckland, Melbourne, Singapore and Toronto
and distributed in the United States of America
by Heinemann, a division of Reed Elsevier Inc.
361 Hanover Street, Portsmouth, New Hampshire
NH 03801 3959

Blasted first published in 1995 by Methuen Drama in
Frontline Intelligence 2 copyright © 1995 by Sarah Kane
Phaedra's Love copyright © 1996 by Sarah Kane
The author has asserted her moral rights

ISBN 0 413 70940 X

A CIP catalogue record for this book is available from the
British Library

Typeset by Wilmaset Ltd, Birkenhead, Wirral
Printed in Great Britain by Cox & Wyman Ltd, Reading,
Berkshire

Contents

Blasted

For Vincent O'Connell, with thanks

Blasted was first performed at the Royal Court Theatre Upstairs, London, on 12 January 1995. The cast was as follows:

Ian	Pip Donaghy
Cate	Kate Ashfield
Soldier	Dermot Kerrigan

Directed by James Macdonald
Designed by Franziska Wilcken
Lighting by Jon Linstrum
Sound by Paul Arditti

Characters

Ian
Cate
Soldier

Scene One

A very expensive hotel room in Leeds — the kind that is so expensive it could be anywhere in the world.

There is a large double bed.
A mini-bar and champagne on ice.
A telephone.
A large bouquet of flowers.
Two doors — one is the entrance from the corridor, the other leads off to the bathroom.

Two people enter — **Ian** *and* **Cate**.

Ian *is 45, Welsh born but lived in Leeds much of his life and picked up the accent.*

Cate *is 21, a lower-middle-class Southerner with a south London accent and a stutter when under stress.*

They enter.

Cate *stops at the door amazed at the classiness of the room.*
Ian *comes in, throws a small pile of newspapers on the bed, goes straight to the mini-bar and pours himself a large gin.*
He looks briefly out of the window at the street, then turns back to the room.

Ian   I've shat in better places than this.

He gulps down the gin.

> I stink.
> You want a bath?

Cate   (*shakes her head*)

Ian *goes into the bathroom and we hear him run the water. He comes back in with only a towel around his waist and a revolver in his hand. He checks it is loaded and puts it under his pillow.*

Ian   Tip that wog when he brings up the sandwiches.

He leaves fifty pence and goes into the bathroom.
Cate *comes into the room. She puts her bag down and bounces on the*

bed. She goes around the room, looking in every drawer, touching everything. She smells the flowers and smiles.

Cate   Lovely.

Ian *comes back in, hair wet, towel around his waist, drying himself off.*
He stops and looks at **Cate** *a moment, who is sucking her thumb.*
He goes back in the bathroom where he dresses.
We hear him coughing terribly in the bathroom.
He spits in the sink and re-enters.

Cate   You all right?

Ian   It's nothing.

He pours himself another gin, this time with tonic, ice and lemon, and sips it at a more normal pace.
He collects his gun and puts it in his under arm holster.
He smiles at **Cate**.

Ian   I'm glad you've come. Didn't think you would.

He offers her champagne.

Cate   (*shakes her head*) I was worried.

Ian   This? (*He indicates his chest.*) Don't matter.

Cate   I didn't mean that. You sounded unhappy.

Ian   (*pops the champagne. He pours them both a glass*)

Cate   What we celebrating?

Ian   (*doesn't answer. He goes to the window and looks out*)
Hate this city. Stinks. Wogs and Pakis taking over.

Cate   You shouldn't call them that.

Ian   Why not?

Cate   It's not very nice.

Ian   You a nigger-lover?

Cate   Ian, don't.

Ian   You like our coloured brethren?

Cate   Don't mind them.

Ian   Grow up.

Cate   There's Indians at the day centre where my brother goes. They're really polite.

Ian   So they should be.

Cate   He's friends with some of them.

Ian   Retard, isn't he?

Cate   No, he's got learning difficulties.

Ian   Aye. Spaz.

Cate   No he's not.

Ian   Glad my son's not a Joey.

Cate   Don't c- call him that.

Ian   Your mother I feel sorry for. Two of you like it.

Cate   Like wh- what?

Ian *looks at her, deciding whether or not to continue. He decides against it.*

Ian   You know I love you.

Cate   (*smiles a big smile, friendly and non-sexual*)

Ian   Don't want you ever to leave.

Cate   I'm here for the night.

Ian *drinks. She's made her point.*

Ian   Sweating again. Stink.
You ever thought of getting married?

Cate   Who'd marry me?

Ian   I would.

Cate   I couldn't.

Ian   You don't love me. I don't blame you, I wouldn't.

Cate   I couldn't leave mum.

Ian   Have to one day.

Cate   Why?

Ian   (*opens his mouth to answer but can't think of one*)

There is a knock at the door.
Ian *starts, and* **Cate** *goes to answer it.*

Ian   Don't.

Cate   Why not?

Ian   I said.

He takes his gun from the holster and goes to the door.
He listens.
Nothing.

Cate   (*giggles*)

Ian   Shh.

He listens.
Still nothing.

Ian   Probably the wog with the sarnies. Open it.

Cate *opens the door.*
There's no one there, just a tray of sandwiches on the floor.
She brings them in and examines them.

Cate   Ham. Don't believe it.

Ian   (*takes a sandwich and eats it*) Champagne?

Cate   (*shakes her head*)

Ian   Got something against ham?

Cate   Dead meat. Blood. Can't eat an animal.

Ian   No one would know.

Cate   No, I can't, I actually can't, I'd puke all over the place.

Ian   It's only a pig.

Cate   I'm hungry.

Ian   Have one of these.

Cate   I CAN'T.

Ian   I'll take you out for an Indian.
Jesus, what's this? Cheese.

Cate *beams.*
She separates the cheese sandwiches from the ham ones, and eats.
Ian *watches her.*

Ian   Don't like your clothes.

Cate   (*looks down at her clothes*)

Ian   You look like a lesbos.

Cate   What's that?

Ian   Don't look very sexy, that's all.

Cate   Oh. (*She continues to eat.*) Don't like your clothes either.

Ian   (*looks down at his clothes.*
Then gets up, takes them all off, and stands in front of her, naked)
Put your mouth on me.

Cate   (*stares. Then bursts out laughing*)

Ian   No? Fine.
Because I stink?

Cate   (*laughs even more*)

Ian *attempts to dress, but fumbles with embarrassment.*
He gathers his clothes and goes into the bathroom where he dresses.
Cate *eats, and giggles over the sandwiches.*
Ian *returns, fully dressed.*
He picks up his gun, unloads and reloads it.

Ian   You got a job yet?

Cate   No.

Ian   Still screwing the taxpayer.

Cate   Mum gives me money.

Ian   When are you going to stand on your own feet?

Cate   I've applied for a job at an advertising agency.

Ian   (*laughs genuinely*) No chance.

Cate   Why not?

Ian   (*stops laughing and looks at her*)
Cate. You're stupid. You're never going to get a job.

Cate   I am. I am not.

Ian   See.

Cate   St- stop it. You're doing it d- deliberately.

Ian   Doing what?

Cate   C- confusing me.

Ian   No, I'm talking, you're just too thick to understand.

Cate   I am not, I am not.

Cate *begins to tremble.* **Ian** *is laughing.*
Cate *faints.*
Ian *stops laughing and stares at her motionless body.*

Ian   Cate?

He turns her over and lifts up her eyelids.
He doesn't know what to do.
He gets a glass of gin and dabs some on her face.
Cate *sits bolt upright, eyes open but still unconscious.*

Ian   Fucking Jesus.

Cate *bursts out laughing, unnaturally, hysterically, uncontrollably.*

Ian   Stop fucking about.

Cate *collapses again and lies still.*
Ian *stands by helplessly.*
After a few moments, **Cate** *comes round as if waking up in the morning.*

Ian   What the Christ was that?

Cate   Have to tell her.

Ian   Cate?

Cate   She's in danger.

She closes her eyes and slowly comes back to normal.
She looks at **Ian** *and smiles.*

Ian   What now?

Cate   Did I faint?

Ian   That was real?

Cate   Happens all the time.

Ian   What, fits?

Cate   Since dad came back.

Ian   Does it hurt?

Cate   I'll grow out of it the doctor says.

Ian   How do you feel?

Cate   (*smiles*)

Ian   Thought you were dead.

Cate   Suppose that's what it's like.

Ian   Don't do it again, fucking scared me.

Cate   Don't know much about it, I just go. Can be away for minutes or months sometimes, then I come back just where I was.

Ian   It's terrible.

Cate   I didn't go far.

Ian   What if you didn't come round?

Cate   Wouldn't know. I'd stay there.

Ian   Can't stand it.

Cate   What?

Ian   Death. Not being.

He goes to the mini-bar and pours himself another large gin and lights a cigarette.

Cate   You fall asleep and then you wake up.

Ian   How do you know?

Cate   Why don't you give up smoking?

Ian   (*laughs*)

Cate   You should. They'll make you ill.

Ian   Too late for that.

Cate   Whenever I think of you it's with a cigarette and a gin.

Ian   Good.

Cate   They make your clothes smell.

Ian   Don't forget my breath.

Cate   Imagine what your lungs must look like.

Ian   Don't need to imagine. I've seen.

Cate   When?

Ian   Last year. When I came round, surgeon brought in this lump of rotting pork, stank. My lung.

Cate   He took it out?

Ian   Other one's the same now.

Cate   But you'll die.

Ian   Aye.

Cate   Please stop smoking.

Ian   Won't make any difference.

Cate   Can't they do something?

Ian   No. It's not like your brother, look after him he'll be all right.

Cate   They die young.

Ian   I'm fucked.

Cate   Can't you get a transplant?

Ian   Don't be stupid. They give them to people with a life. Kids.

Cate   People die in accidents all the time. They must have some spare.

Ian   Why? What for? Keep me alive to die of cirrhosis in three months time.

Cate   You're making it worse, speeding it up.

Ian   Enjoy myself while I'm here.

(*He inhales deeply on his cigarette and swallows the last of the gin neat.*)

[I'll] Call that coon, get some more sent up.

Cate   (*shakes*)

Ian   Wonder if the conker understands English.

He notices **Cate**'s *distress and cuddles her. He kisses her. She pulls away and wipes her mouth.*

Cate   Don't put your tongue in, I don't like it.

Ian   Sorry.

The telephone rings loudly. **Ian** *starts, then answers it.*

Ian   Hello?

Cate   Who is it?

Ian   (*covers the mouthpiece*) Shh.

(*Into the mouthpiece.*) Got it here.

(*He takes a notebook from the pile of newspapers and reads down the phone.*)

A serial killer slaughtered British tourist Samantha Scrace in a sick murder ritual comma, police revealed yesterday point new par. The bubbly nineteen-year-old from Leeds was among seven victims found buried in identical triangular tombs in an isolated New Zealand forest point new par. Each had been stabbed more than twenty times and placed face down comma, hands bound behind their backs point new par. Caps up, ashes at the site showed the maniac had stayed to cook a meal, caps down point new par. Samantha comma, a beautiful redhead with dreams of becoming a model comma, was on the trip of a lifetime after finishing her A levels last year point. Samantha's heartbroken mum said yesterday colon quoting, we pray the police will come up with something dash, anything comma, soon point still quoting. The sooner this lunatic is brought to justice the better point end quote new par. The Foreign Office warned tourists down under to take extra care point. A spokesman said colon quoting, common sense is the best rule point end quote, copy ends.

(*He listens. Then he laughs.*)

Exactly.

(*He listens.*)

That one again, I went to see her. Scouse tart, spread her legs. No. Forget it. Tears and lies, not worth the space. No.

He presses a button on the phone to connect him to room service.

Ian   Tosser.

Cate   How do they know you're here?

Ian   Told them.

Cate   Why?

Ian   In case they needed me.

Cate   Silly. We came here to be away from them.

Ian   Thought you'd like this. Nice hotel. (*Into the mouthpiece.*) Bring a bottle of gin up, son.

He puts the phone down.

Cate   We always used to go to yours.

Ian   That was years ago. You've grown up.

Cate   (*smiles*)

Ian   I'm not well any more.

Cate   (*stops smiling*)

Ian kisses her.
She responds.
He puts his hand inside her shirt and moves it towards her breast.
With the other hand he undoes his trousers and starts masturbating.
He begins to undo her shirt.
She pushes him away.

Cate   Ian, d- don't.

Ian   What?

Cate   I don't w- want to do this.

Ian   Yes you do.

Cate   I don't.

Ian   Why not? You're nervous, that's all.

He starts to kiss her again.

Cate   I t- t- t- t- t- t- t- told you. I really like you but I c- c- c- c- can't do this.

Ian   (*kissing her*) Shhh. (*He starts to undo her trousers.*)

Cate panics.
She starts to tremble and make inarticulate crying sounds.
Ian stops, frightened of bringing another 'fit' on.

Ian   All right, Cate, it's all right. We don't have to do anything.

He strokes her face until she has calmed down.
She sucks her thumb. Then.

Ian   That wasn't very fair.

Cate   What?

Ian   Leaving me hanging, making a prick of myself.

Cate   I f- f- felt –

Ian   Don't pity me, Cate. You don't have to fuck me 'cause I'm dying, but don't push your cunt in my face then take it away 'cause I stick my tongue out.

Cate   I- I- Ian.

Ian   What's the m- m- matter?

Cate   I k- k- kissed you, that's all. I l- l- like you.

Ian   Don't give me a hard-on if you're not going to finish me off. It hurts.

Cate   I'm sorry.

Ian   Can't switch it on and off like that. If I don't come my cock aches.

Cate   I didn't mean it.

Ian   Shit. (*He appears to be in considerable pain.*)

Cate   I'm sorry. I am. I won't do it again.

Ian, *apparently still in pain, takes her hand and grasps it around his penis, keeping his own hand over the top.*
Like this, he masturbates until he comes with some genuine pain.
He releases **Cate**'*s hand and she withdraws it.*

Cate   Is it better?

Ian   (*nods*)

Cate   I'm sorry.

Ian   Don't worry.
Can we make love tonight?

Cate   No.

Ian Why not?

Cate I'm not your girlfriend any more.

Ian Will you be my girlfriend again?

Cate I can't.

Ian Why not?

Cate I told Shaun I'd be his.

Ian Have you slept with him?

Cate No.

Ian Slept with me before. You're more mine than his.

Cate I'm not.

Ian What was that about then, wanking me off?

Cate I d- d- d- d-

Ian Sorry. Pressure, pressure. I love you, that's all.

Cate You were horrible to me.

Ian I wasn't.

Cate Stopped phoning me, never said why.

Ian It was difficult, Cate.

Cate Because I haven't got a job?

Ian No, pet, not that.

Cate Because of my brother?

Ian No, no, Cate. Leave it now.

Cate That's not fair.

Ian I said leave it.

He reaches for his gun.
There is a knock at the door.
Ian *starts, then goes to answer it.*

Ian   I'm not going to hurt you, just leave it. And keep quiet. It'll only be Sooty after something.

Cate   Andrew.

Ian   What do you want to know a conker's name for?

Cate   I thought he was nice.

Ian   After a bit of black meat, eh? Won't do it with me but you'll go with a whodat.

Cate   You're horrible.

Ian   Cate, love. I'm trying to look after you. Stop you getting hurt.

Cate   You hurt me.

Ian   No, I love you.

Cate   Stopped loving me.

Ian   I've told you to leave that.
        Now.

He kisses her passionately, then goes to the door.
When his back is turned, **Cate** *wipes her mouth.*
Ian *opens the door. There is a bottle of gin outside on a tray.*
Ian *brings it in and stands, unable to decide between gin and champagne.*

Cate   Have champagne, better for you.

Ian   Don't want it better for me.

Cate   You'll die quicker.

Ian   Thanks. Don't it scare you?

Cate   What?

Ian   Death.

Cate   Whose?

Ian   Yours.

Cate   Only for mum. She'd be unhappy if I died. And my brother.

Ian   You're young.
When I was your age –
Now.

Cate   Will you have to go to hospital?

Ian   Nothing they can do.

Cate   Does Stella know?

Ian   What would I want to tell her for?

Cate   You were married.

Ian   So?

Cate   She'd want to know.

Ian   So she can throw a party at the coven.

Cate   She wouldn't do that. What about Matthew?

Ian   What about Matthew?

Cate   Have you told him?

Ian   I'll send him an invite for the funeral.

Cate   He'll be upset.

Ian   He hates me.

Cate   He doesn't.

Ian   He fucking does.

Cate   Are you upset?

Ian   Yes. His mother's a lesbos. Am I not preferable to that?

Cate   Perhaps she's a nice person.

Ian   She don't carry a gun.

Cate   I expect that's it.

Ian   I loved Stella till she became a witch and fucked off with a dyke, and I love you, though you've got the potential.

Cate   For what?

Ian   Sucking gash.

Cate   (*utters an inarticulate sound*)

Ian   You ever had a fuck with a woman?

Cate   No.

Ian   Do you want to?

Cate   Don't think so. Have you? With a man.

Ian   You think I'm a cocksucker? You've seen me. (*He vaguely indicates his groin.*) How can you think that?

Cate   I don't. I asked. You asked me.

Ian   You dress like a lesbos. I don't dress like a cocksucker.

Cate   What do they dress like?

Ian   Hitler was wrong about the Jews who have they hurt the queers he should have gone for scum them and the wogs and fucking football fans send a bomber over Elland Road finish them off.

He pours champagne and toasts the idea.

Cate   I like football.

Ian   Why?

Cate   It's good.

Ian   And when was the last time you went to a football match?

Cate   Saturday. United beat Liverpool 2–0.

Ian   Didn't you get stabbed?

Cate   Why should I?

Ian   That's what football's about. It's not fancy footwork and scoring goals. It's tribalism.

Cate I like it.

Ian You would. About your level.

Cate I go to Elland Road sometimes. Would you bomb me?

Ian What do you want to ask a question like that for?

Cate Would you though?

Ian Don't be thick.

Cate But would you?

Ian Haven't got a bomber.

Cate Shoot me, then. Could you do that?

Ian Cate.

Cate Do you think it's hard to shoot someone?

Ian Easy as shitting blood.

Cate Could you shoot me?

Ian Could you shoot me stop asking that could you shoot me you could shoot me.

Cate I don't think so.

Ian If I hurt you.

Cate Don't think you would.

Ian But if.

Cate No, you're soft.

Ian With people I love.

He stares at her, considering making a pass.
She smiles back, friendly.

Ian What's this job, then?

Cate Personal Assistant.

Ian Who to?

Cate Don't know.

Ian   Who did you write the letter to?

Cate   Sir or madam.

Ian   You have to know who you're writing to.

Cate   It didn't say.

Ian   How much?

Cate   What?

Ian   Money. How much do you get paid.

Cate   Mum said it was a lot. I don't mind about that as long as I can go out sometimes.

Ian   Don't despise money. You got it easy.

Cate   I haven't got any money.

Ian   No and you haven't got kids to bring up neither.

Cate   Not yet.

Ian   Don't even think about it. Who would have children. You have kids, they grow up, they hate you and you die.

Cate   I don't hate mum.

Ian   You still need her.

Cate   You think I'm stupid. I'm not stupid.

Ian   I worry, that's all.

Cate   Can look after myself.

Ian   Like me.

Cate   No.

Ian   You hate me, don't you.

Cate   You shouldn't have that gun.

Ian   May need it.

Cate   What for?

Ian   (*drinks*)

Cate Can't imagine it.

Ian What?

Cate You. Shooting someone. You wouldn't kill anything.

Ian (*drinks*)

Cate Have you ever shot anyone?

Ian Your mind.

Cate Have you though?

Ian Leave it now, Cate.

She takes the warning.
Ian *kisses her and lights a cigarette.*

Ian When I'm with you I can't think about anything else.
You take me to another place.

Cate It's like that when I have a fit.

Ian Just you.

Cate The world don't exist, not like this. Looks the same
but –
Time slows down.
A dream I get stuck in, can't do nothing about it.
One time –

Ian Make love to me.

Cate Blocks out everything else.
Once –

Ian [I'll] Make love to you.

Cate It's like that when I touch myself.

Ian *is embarrassed.*

Cate Just before I'm wondering what it'll be like, and just
after I'm thinking about the next one, but just as it happens
it's lovely, I don't think of nothing else.

Ian   Like the first cigarette of the day.

Cate   That's bad for you though.

Ian   Stop talking now, you don't know anything about it.

Cate   Don't need to.

Ian   Don't know nothing. That's why I love you, want to make love to you.

Cate   But you can't.

Ian   Why not?

Cate   I don't want to.

Ian   Why did you come here?

Cate   You sounded unhappy.

Ian   Make me happy.

Cate   I can't.

Ian   Please.

Cate   No.

Ian   Why not?

Cate   Can't.

Ian   Can.

Cate   How.

Ian   You know.

Cate   Don't.

Ian   Please.

Cate   No.

Ian   I love you.

Cate   I don't love you.

Ian *turns away.*
He sees the bouquet of flowers and picks them up.

Ian   These are for you.

Blackout.

The sound of spring rain.

Scene Two

The same.

Very early the following morning.
Bright and sunny — it's going to be a very hot day.
The bouquet of flowers is now ripped apart and scattered around the room.

Cate *is still asleep.*
Ian *is awake, glancing through the newspapers.*

Ian *goes to the mini-bar. It is empty.*
He finds the bottle of gin under the bed and pours half of what is left into a glass.
He stands looking out of the window at the street.
He takes the first sip and is overcome with pain.
He waits for it to pass, but it doesn't. It gets worse.
Ian *clutches his side — it becomes extreme.*
He begins to cough, and experiences intense pain in his chest, each cough tearing at his lung.

Cate *wakes and watches* **Ian**.

Ian *drops to his knees, puts the glass down carefully, and gives in to the pain.*
It looks very much as if he is dying.
His heart, lung, liver and kidneys are all under attack, and he is making involuntary crying sounds.

Just at the moment when it seems he cannot survive this, it begins to ease.
Very slowly, the pain decreases until it has all gone.

Ian *is a crumpled heap on the floor.*

He looks up and sees **Cate** *watching him.*

Cate   Cunt.

Ian *gets up slowly, picks up the glass and drinks.*
He lights his first cigarette of the day.

Ian   I'm having a shower.

Cate   It's only six o'clock.

Ian   Want one?

Cate   Not with you.

Ian   Suit yourself. Cigarette?

Cate *makes a noise of disgust.*
They are silent.

Ian *stands, smoking and drinking neat gin.*
When he's sufficiently numbed, he comes and goes between the bedroom
and the bathroom, undressing and collecting discarded towels.
He stops, towel around his waist, gun in hand, and looks at **Cate**.
She is staring at him with hate.

Ian   Don't worry, I'll be dead soon.

   (*He tosses the gun onto the bed.*)

   Have a pop.

Cate *doesn't move.*
Ian *waits, then chuckles and goes into the bathroom.*
We hear the shower running.

Cate *stares at the gun.*
She gets up very slowly and dresses.
She packs her bag.
She picks up **Ian**'s *leather jacket and smells it.*
She rips the arms off at the seams.
She picks up his gun and examines it.
We hear **Ian** *coughing up in the bathroom.*
Cate *puts the gun down and he comes in.*
He dresses. He looks at the gun.

Ian   No?

(*He chuckles, unloads and reloads the gun and tucks it in his holster.*)

We're one, yes?

Cate (*sneers*)

Ian We're one.
Coming down for breakfast? It's paid for.

Cate Choke on it.

Ian Sarky little tart this morning, aren't we?

He picks up his jacket and begins to put it on.
He stares at the damage, then looks at **Cate**.
A beat, and then she goes for him, slapping him around the head hard and fast.
He wrestles her onto the bed, her still kicking, punching and biting.
She takes the gun from his holster and points it at his groin.
He backs off rapidly.

Ian Easy, easy, that's a loaded gun.

Cate I d- d- d- d- d- d- d- d- d-

Ian Catie, come on.

Cate d- d- d- d- d- d- d- d- d- d-

Ian You don't want an accident. Think about your mum.
And your brother. What would they think?

Cate I d- d- d- d- d- d- d- d- d- d- d- d- d-

Cate *trembles and starts gasping for air. She faints.*
Ian *goes to her, takes the gun and puts it back in the holster.*
He lies her on the bed, on her back.
He puts the gun to her head, lies between her legs, and simulates sex.
As he comes, **Cate** *sits bolt upright with a shout.*
Ian *moves away, unsure what to do, pointing the gun at her from behind.*
She laughs hysterically, as before, but doesn't stop.
She laughs and laughs and laughs until she isn't laughing any more,
she's crying her heart out.
She collapses again and lies still.

Ian   Cate? Catie?

Ian *puts the gun away.*
He kisses her and she comes round.
She stares at him.

Ian   You back?

Cate   Liar.

Ian *doesn't know if this means yes or no, so he just waits.*
Cate *closes her eyes for a few seconds, then opens them.*

Ian   Cate?

Cate   Want to go home now.

Ian   It's not even seven. There won't be a train.

Cate   I'll wait at the station.

Ian   It's raining.

Cate   It's not.

Ian   Want you to stay here. Till after breakfast at least.

Cate   No.

Ian   Cate. After breakfast.

Cate   No.

Ian *locks the door and pockets the key.*

Ian   I love you.

Cate   I don't want to stay.

Ian   Please.

Cate   Don't want to.

Ian   You make me feel safe.

Cate   Nothing to be scared of.

Ian   I'll order breakfast.

Cate   Not hungry.

Ian   (*lights a cigarette*)

Cate   How can you smoke on an empty stomach?

Ian   It's not empty. There's gin in it.

Cate   Why can't I go home?

Ian   (*thinks*)
It's too dangerous.

Outside, a car backfires – there is an enormous bang.
Ian throws himself flat on the floor.

Cate   (*laughs*) It's only a car.

Ian   You. You're fucking thick.

Cate   I'm not. You're scared of things when there's nothing to be scared of. What's thick about not being scared of cars?

Ian   I'm not scared of cars. I'm scared of dying.

Cate   A car won't kill you. Not from out there.
Not unless you ran out in front of it.

(*She kisses him.*)

What's scaring you?

Ian   Thought it was a gun.

Cate   (*kissing his neck*) Who'd have a gun?

Ian   Me.

Cate   (*undoing his shirt*) You're in here.

Ian   Someone like me.

Cate   (*kissing his chest*) Why would they shoot at you?

Ian   Revenge.

Cate   (*runs her hands down his back*)

Ian   For things I've done.

Cate   (*massaging his neck*) Tell me.

Ian   Tapped my phone.

Cate   (*kisses the back of his neck*)

Ian   Talk to someone and I know I'm being listened to.
I'm sorry I stopped calling you but –

Cate   (*strokes his stomach and kisses between his shoulder blades*)

Ian   Got angry when you said you loved me, talking soft on
the phone, people listening to that.

Cate   (*kissing his back*) Tell me.

Ian   In before you know it.

Cate   (*licks his back*)

Ian   Signed the Official Secrets Act, shouldn't be telling you
this.

Cate   (*claws and scratches his back*)

Ian   Don't want to get you into trouble.

Cate   (*bites his back*)

Ian   Think they're trying to kill me. Served my purpose.

Cate   (*pushes him onto his back*)

Ian   Done the jobs they asked. Because I love this land.

Cate   (*sucks his nipples*)

Ian   Stood at stations, listened to conversations and given
the nod.

Cate   (*undoes his trousers*)

Ian   Driving jobs. Picking people up, disposing of bodies,
the lot.

Cate   (*begins to perform oral sex on* **Ian**)

Ian   Said you were dangerous.

So I stopped.

Didn't want you in any danger.

But

Had to call you again

Missed

This

Now

I do

The real job

I

Am

A

Killer

On the word 'killer' he comes.
As soon as **Cate** *hears the word she bites his penis as hard as she can.*
Ian*'s cry of pleasure turns into a scream of pain.*
He tries to pull away but **Cate** *holds on with her teeth.*
He hits her and she lets go.
Ian *lies in pain, unable to speak.*
Cate *spits frantically, trying to get every trace of him out of her mouth.*
She goes to the bathroom and we hear her cleaning her teeth.
Ian *examines himself. He is still in one piece.*
Cate *returns.*

Cate   You should resign.

Ian   Don't work like that.

Cate   Will they come here?

Ian   I don't know.

Cate   (*begins to panic*)

Ian   Don't start that again.

Cate   I c- c- c- c- c-

Ian   Cate, I'll shoot you myself you don't stop.
I told you because I love you, not to scare you.

Cate You don't.

Ian Don't argue I do. And you love me.

Cate No more.

Ian Loved me last night.

Cate I didn't want to do it.

Ian Thought you liked that.

Cate No.

Ian Made enough noise.

Cate It was hurting.

Ian Went down on Stella all the time, didn't hurt her.

Cate You bit me. It's still bleeding.

Ian Is that what this is all about?

Cate You're cruel.

Ian Don't be stupid.

Cate Stop calling me that.

Ian You sleep with someone holding hands and kissing you wank me off then say we can't fuck get into bed but don't want me to touch you what's wrong with you Joey.

Cate I'm not. You're cruel. I wouldn't shoot someone.

Ian Pointed it at me.

Cate Wouldn't shoot.

Ian It's my job. I love this country. I won't see it destroyed by slag.

Cate It's wrong to kill.

Ian Planting bombs and killing little kiddies, that's wrong. That's what they do. Kids like your brother.

Cate It's wrong.

Ian Yes, it is.

Cate   No. You. Doing that.

Ian   When are you going to grow up?

Cate   I don't believe in killing.

Ian   You'll learn.

Cate   No I won't.

Ian   Can't always be taking it backing down letting them think they've got a right turn the other cheek SHIT some things are worth more than that have to be protected from shite.

Cate   I used to love you.

Ian   What's changed?

Cate   You.

Ian   No. Now you see me. That's all.

Cate   You're a nightmare.

She shakes.
Ian watches a while, then hugs her.
She is still shaking so he hugs tightly to stop her.

Cate   That hurts.

Ian   Sorry.

He hugs her less tightly.
He has a coughing fit.
He spits into his handkerchief and waits for the pain to subside.
Then he lights a cigarette.

Ian   How you feeling?

Cate   I ache.

Ian   (*nods*)

Cate   Everywhere.
          I stink of you.

Ian   You want a bath?

Cate begins to cough and retch.
She puts her fingers down her throat and produces a hair.
She holds it up and looks at **Ian** *in disgust. She spits.*
Ian *goes into the bathroom and turns on one of the bath taps.*
Cate stares out of the window.
Ian *returns.*

Cate   Looks like there's a war on.

Ian   Turning into wogland.
You coming to Leeds again?

Cate   Twenty-sixth.

Ian   Will you come and see me?

Cate   I'm going to the football.

She goes to the bathroom.
Ian *picks up the phone.*

Ian   Two English breakfasts, son.

He finishes the remainder of the gin.
Cate *returns.*

Cate   I can't piss. It's just blood.

Ian   Drink lots of water.

Cate   Or shit. It hurts.

Ian   It'll heal.

There is a knock at the door. They both jump.

Cate   DON'T ANSWER IT DON'T ANSWER IT DON'T
ANSWER IT

She dives on the bed and puts her head under the pillow.

Ian   Cate, shut up.

He pulls the pillow off and puts the gun to her head.

Cate   Do it. Go on, shoot me. Can't be no worse than what
you've done already. Shoot me if you want, then turn it on
yourself and do the world a favour.

Ian   (*stares at her*)

Cate   I'm not scared of you, Ian. Go on.

Ian   (*gets off her*)

Cate   (*laughs*)

Ian   Answer the door and suck the cunt's cock.

Cate *tries to open the door. It is locked.*
Ian *throws the key at her. She opens the door.*
The breakfasts are outside on a tray. She brings them in.
Ian *locks the door.*
Cate *stares at the food.*

Cate   Sausages. Bacon.

Ian   Sorry. Forgot. Swap your meat for my tomatoes and mushrooms. And toast.

Cate   (*begins to retch*) The smell.

Ian *takes a sausage off the plate and stuffs it in his mouth, and keeps a rasher of bacon in his hand.*
He puts the tray of food under the bed with a towel over it.

Ian   Will you stay another day?

Cate   I'm having a bath and going home.

She picks up her bag and goes into the bathroom, closing the door.
We hear the other bath tap being turned on.
There are two loud knocks at the outer door.
Ian *draws his gun, goes to the door and listens.*
The door is tried from outside. It is locked.
There are two more loud knocks.

Ian   Who's there?

Silence.
Then two more loud knocks.

Ian   Who's there?

Silence.
Then two more knocks.

Ian *looks at the door.*
Then he knocks twice.
Silence.
Then two more knocks from outside.

Ian *thinks.*
Then he knocks three times.

Silence.
Three knocks from outside.

Ian *knocks once.*
One knock from outside.

Ian *knocks twice.*
Two knocks.

Ian *puts his gun back in the holster and unlocks the door.*

Ian   (*under his breath*) Speak the Queen's English fucking nigger.

He opens the door.
*Outside is a **Soldier** with a sniper's rifle.*
Ian *tries to push the door shut and draw his revolver.*
*The **Soldier** pushes the door open and takes **Ian**'s gun easily.*
The two stand, both surprised, staring at each other.
Eventually.

Soldier   What's that?

Ian *looks down and realises he is still holding a rasher of bacon.*

Ian   Pig.

*The **Soldier** holds out his hand.*
Ian *gives him the bacon and he eats it quickly, rind and all.*
*The **Soldier** wipes his mouth.*

Soldier   Got any more?

Ian   No.

Soldier   Got any more?

Ian   I –
No.

Soldier   Got any more?

Ian   (*points to the tray under the bed*)

The **Soldier** *bends down carefully, never taking his eyes or rifle off* **Ian***, and takes the tray from under the bed.*
He straightens up and glances down at the food.

Soldier   Two.

Ian   I was hungry.

Soldier   I bet.

He sits on the edge of the bed and very quickly devours both breakfasts.
He sighs with relief and burps.
He nods towards the bathroom.

Soldier   She in there?

Ian   Who?

Soldier   I can smell the sex.

(*He begins to search the room.*)

You a journalist?

Ian   I –

Soldier   Passport.

Ian   What for?

Soldier   (*looks at him*)

Ian   In the jacket.

The **Soldier** *is searching a chest of drawers.*
He finds a pair of **Cate***'s knickers and holds them up with a smile.*

Soldier   Hers?

Ian   (*doesn't answer*)

Soldier   Or yours.

(*He closes his eyes and rubs them gently over his face, smelling with pleasure.*)

What's she like?

Ian (*doesn't answer*)

Soldier Is she soft?
Is she – ?

Ian (*doesn't answer*)

The **Soldier** *puts* **Cate**'s *knickers in his pocket and goes to the bathroom.*
He knocks on the door. No answer.
He tries the door. It is locked. He forces it and goes in.
Ian *waits, in a panic.*
We hear the bath taps being turned off.
Ian *looks out of the window.*

Ian Jesus Lord.

The **Soldier** *returns.*

Soldier Gone. Taking a risk. Lot of bastard soldiers out there.

Ian *looks in the bathroom.* **Cate** *isn't there.*
The **Soldier** *looks in* **Ian**'s *jacket pockets and takes his keys, money and passport.*

Soldier (*reading the passport*) Ian Jones, occupation journalist.

Ian Oi.

Soldier Oi.

They stare at each other.

Ian If you've come to shoot me –

The **Soldier** *reaches out to touch* **Ian**'s *face.*

Ian You taking the piss?

Soldier Me?

(*He smiles.*)

Our town now.

(*He stands on the bed and urinates over the pillows.*)

Ian *is disgusted.*

There is a blinding light, then a huge explosion.

Blackout.

The sound of summer rain.

Scene Three

The hotel has been blasted by a mortar bomb.

There is a large hole in one of the walls, and everything is covered in dust which is still falling.

The **Soldier** *is unconscious, rifle still in hand.*
He has dropped **Ian**'s *gun which lies between them.*

Ian *lies very still, eyes open.*

Ian   Mum?

Silence.
The **Soldier** *wakes and turns his eyes and rifle on* **Ian** *with the minimum possible movement. He instinctively runs his free hand over his limbs and body to check that he is still in one piece. He is.*

Soldier   The drink.

Ian *looks around.*
There is a bottle of gin lying next to him with the lid off.
He holds it up to the light.

Ian   Empty.

The **Soldier** *takes the bottle and drinks the last mouthful.*

Ian   (*chuckles*) Worse than me.

Soldier   (*holds the bottle up and shakes it over his mouth, catching any remaining drops*)

Ian   (*finds his cigarettes in his shirt pocket and lights up*)

Soldier   Give us a cig.

Ian   Why?

Soldier   'Cause I've got a gun and you haven't.

Ian   (*considers the logic.*
Then takes a single cigarette out of the packet and tosses
it at the **Soldier**)

Soldier   (*picks up the cigarette and puts it in his mouth.*
Looks at **Ian**, *waiting for a light*)

Ian   (*looks back, considering*)

Soldier   (*waits*)

Ian   (*holds out his cigarette*)

Soldier   (*leans forward, touching the tip of his cigarette against the*
lit one, eyes always on **Ian**.

He smokes.)

Never met an Englishman with a gun before, most
of them don't know what a gun is. You a soldier?

Ian   Of sorts.

Soldier   Which side, if you can remember.

Ian   Don't know what the sides are here. Don't know
where . . .

(*He trails off, confused, and looks at the* **Soldier**.)

Think I might be drunk.

Soldier   No. It's real.

(*Picks up the revolver and examines it.*)

Come to fight for us?

Ian   No, I –

Soldier   No, course not. English.

Ian   I'm Welsh.

Soldier   Sound English, fucking accent.

Ian   I live there.

Soldier   Foreigner?

Ian   English and Welsh is the same. British. I'm not an import.

Soldier   What's fucking Welsh, never heard of it.

Ian   Come over from God knows where have their kids and call them English they're not English born in England don't make you English.

Soldier   Welsh as in Wales?

Ian   It's attitude.

(*He turns away.*)

Look at the state of my fucking jacket. The bitch.

Soldier   Your girlfriend did that, angry was she?

Ian   She's not my girlfriend.

Soldier   What, then?

Ian   Mind your fucking own.

Soldier   Haven't been here long have you.

Ian   So?

Soldier   Learn some manners, Ian.

Ian   Don't call me that.

Soldier   What shall I call you?

Ian   Nothing.

Silence.
The **Soldier** *looks at* **Ian** *for a very long time, saying nothing.*
Ian *is uncomfortable.*
Eventually.

Ian   What?

Soldier   Nothing.

Silence.
Ian *is uneasy again.*

Ian   My name's Ian.

Soldier   I
            Am
            Dying to make love, Ian.

Ian   (*looks at him*)

Soldier   You got a girlfriend?

Ian   (*doesn't answer*)

Soldier   I have. Col. Fucking beautiful.

Ian   Cate –

Soldier   Close my eyes and think about her.
            She's –
            She's –
            She's –
            She's –
            She's –
            She's –
            She's –
            When was the last time you – ?

Ian   (*looks at him*)

Soldier   When? I know it was recent, smell it, remember.

Ian   Last night. I think.

Soldier   Good?

Ian   Don't know. I was pissed. Probably not.

Soldier   Three of us.

Ian   Don't tell me.

Soldier   Went to a house just outside town. All gone. Apart
from a small boy hiding in the corner. One of the others took

him outside. Lay him on the ground and shot him through the legs. Heard crying in the basement. Went down. Three men and four women. Called the others. They held the men while I fucked the women. Youngest was twelve. Didn't cry, just lay there. Turned her over and –

Then she cried. Made her lick me clean. Closed my eyes and thought of –

Shot her father in the mouth. Brothers shouted. Hung them from the ceiling by their testicles.

Ian Charming.

Soldier Never done that?

Ian No.

Soldier Sure?

Ian I wouldn't forget.

Soldier You would.

Ian Couldn't sleep with myself.

Soldier What about your wife?

Ian I'm divorced.

Soldier Didn't you ever –

Ian No.

Soldier What about that girl, locked herself in the bathroom.

Ian (*doesn't answer*)

Soldier Ah.

Ian You did four in one go, I've only ever done one.

Soldier You killed her?

Ian (*makes a move for his gun*)

Soldier Don't I'll have to shoot you. Then I'd be lonely.

Ian Course I haven't.

Soldier   Why not, don't seem to like her very much.

Ian   I do.
She's . . . a woman.

Soldier   So.

Ian   I've never –
It's not –

Soldier   What?

Ian   (*doesn't answer*)

Soldier   Thought you were a soldier.

Ian   Not like that.

Soldier   Not like that, they're all like that.

Ian   My job –

Soldier   Even me. Have to be.
My girl –
Not going back to her. When I go back.
She's dead, see. Fucking bastard soldier, he –

He stops.
Silence.

Ian   I'm sorry.

Soldier   Why?

Ian   It's terrible.

Soldier   What is?

Ian   Losing someone, a woman, like that.

Soldier   You know, do you?

Ian   I –

Soldier   Like what?

Ian   Like –
You said –
A soldier –

Soldier You're a soldier.

Ian I haven't –

Soldier What if you were ordered to?

Ian Can't imagine it.

Soldier Imagine it.

Ian (*imagines it*)

Soldier In the line of duty. For your country. Wales.

Ian (*imagines harder*)

Soldier Foreign slag.

Ian (*imagines harder. Looks sick*)

Soldier Would you?

Ian (*nods*)

Soldier How.

Ian Quickly. Back of the head. Bam.

Soldier That's all.

Ian It's enough.

Soldier You think?

Ian Yes.

Soldier You never killed anyone.

Ian Fucking have.

Soldier No.

Ian Don't you fucking –

Soldier Couldn't talk like this. You'd know.

Ian Know what?

Soldier Exactly. You don't know.

Ian Know fucking what?

Soldier Stay in the dark.

Ian What? Fucking what? What don't I know?

Soldier You think –

(*He stops and smiles*)

I broke a woman's neck. Stabbed up between her legs, on the fifth stab snapped her spine.

Ian (*looks sick*)

Soldier You couldn't do that.

Ian No.

Soldier You never killed.

Ian Not like that.

Soldier Not
Like
That

Ian I'm not a torturer.

Soldier You're close to them, gun to head. Tie them up, tell them what you're going to do to them, make them wait for it, then . . . what?

Ian Shoot them.

Soldier You haven't got a clue.

Ian What, then?

Soldier You never fucked a man before you killed him?

Ian No.

Soldier Or after?

Ian Course not.

Soldier Why not?

Ian What for, I'm not queer.

Soldier   Col, they buggered her. Cut her throat. Hacked her ears and nose off, nailed them to the front door.

Ian   Enough.

Soldier   Ever seen anything like that?

Ian   Stop.

Soldier   Not in photos?

Ian   Never.

Soldier   Some journalist, that's your job.

Ian   What?

Soldier   Proving it happened. I'm here, got no choice. But you. You should be telling people.

Ian   No one's interested.

Soldier   You can do something, for me –

Ian   No.

Soldier   Course you can.

Ian   I can't do anything.

Soldier   Try.

Ian   I write . . . stories. That's all. Stories. This isn't a story anyone wants to hear.

Soldier   Why not?

Ian   (*takes one of the newspapers from the bed and reads*)

'Kinky car dealer Richard Morris drove two teenage prostitutes into the country, tied them naked to fences and whipped them with a belt before having sex. Morris, from Sheffield, was jailed for three years for unlawful sexual intercourse with one of the girls, aged thirteen.'

(*He tosses the paper away*)

Stories.

Soldier   Doing to them what they done to us, what good is that? At home I'm clean. Like it never happened. Tell them you saw me. Tell them . . . you saw me.

Ian   It's not my job.

Soldier   Whose is it?

Ian   I'm a home journalist, for Yorkshire. I don't cover foreign affairs.

Soldier   Foreign affairs, what you doing here?

Ian   I do other stuff. Shootings and rapes and kids getting fiddled by queer priests and schoolteachers. Not soldiers screwing each other for a patch of land. It has to be . . . personal. Your girlfriend, she's a story. Soft and clean. Not you. Filthy, like the wogs. No joy in a story about blacks who gives a shit? Why bring you to light?

Soldier   You don't know fuck all about me.
I went to school.
I made love with Col.
Bastards killed her, now I'm here.
Now I'm here.

(*He pushes the rifle in* **Ian***'s face.*)

Turn over, Ian.

Ian   Why?

Soldier   Going to fuck you.

Ian   No.

Soldier   Kill you, then.

Ian   Fine.

Soldier   See. Rather be shot than fucked and shot.

Ian   Yes.

Soldier   And now you agree with anything I say.

(He kisses **Ian** *very tenderly on the lips.*
They stare at each other)

You smell like her. Same cigarettes.

He gets up and turns **Ian** *over with one hand.*
He holds the revolver to **Ian**'s *head with the other.*
He pulls down **Ian**'s *trousers, undoes his own and rapes him – eyes*
closed and smelling **Ian**'s *hair.*
The **Soldier** *is crying his heart out.*

Ian's *face registers pain but he is silent.*

When the **Soldier** *has finished he pulls up his trousers and pushes the*
revolver up **Ian**'s *anus.*

Soldier   Bastard pulled the trigger on Col.
What's it like?

Ian   *(tries to answer. He can't)*

Soldier   *(withdraws the gun and sits next to* **Ian***)*

You never fucked by a man before?

Ian   *(doesn't answer)*

Soldier   Didn't think so. It's nothing. Saw thousands of
people packing into trucks like pigs trying to leave town.
Women threw their babies on board hoping someone would
look after them. Crushing each other to death. Insides of
people's heads came out of their eyes. Saw a child most of his
face blown off, young girl I fucked hand up inside her trying
to claw my liquid out, starving man eating his dead wife's leg.
Gun was born here and won't die. Can't get tragic about your
arse. Don't think your Welsh arse is different to any other arse
I fucked. Sure you haven't got any more food, I'm fucking
starving.

Ian   Are you going to kill me?

Soldier   Always looking after your own arse.

The **Soldier** *grips* **Ian**'s *head in his hands.*

He puts his mouth over one of **Ian**'s *eyes, sucks it out, bites it off and eats it.*

He does the same to the other eye.

Soldier   He ate her eyes.
Poor bastard.
Poor love.
Poor fucking bastard.

Blackout.

The sound of autumn rain.

Scene Four

The same.

The **Soldier** *lies close to* **Ian**, *the revolver in his hand. He has blown his own brain out.*

Cate *enters through the bathroom door, soaking wet and carrying a baby. She steps over the* **Soldier** *with a glance.*
Then she sees **Ian**.

Cate   You're a nightmare.

Ian   Cate?

Cate   It won't stop.

Ian   Catie? You here?

Cate   Everyone in town is crying.

Ian   Touch me.

Cate   They can't stop. Soldiers have taken over.

Ian   They've won?

Cate   Most people gave up.

Ian   You seen Matthew?

Cate   No.

Ian   Will you tell him for me?

Cate   He isn't here.

Ian   Tell him –
Tell him –

Cate   No.

Ian   Tell him –

Cate   No.

Ian   Don't know what to tell him.
I'm cold.
Tell him –
You here?

Cate   A woman gave me her baby.

Ian   You come for me, Catie? Punish me or rescue me makes no difference I love you Cate tell him for me do it for me touch me Cate.

Cate   Don't know what to do with it.

Ian   I'm cold.

Cate   Keeps crying.

Ian   Tell him –

Cate   I can't.

Ian   Will you stay with me, Cate?

Cate   No.

Ian   Why not?

Cate   I have to go back soon.

Ian   Shaun know what we did?

Cate   Nothing.

Ian   Better tell him.

Cate   No.

Ian   He'll know. Even if you don't.

Cate   How?

Ian   Smell it. Soiled goods. Don't want it, not when you can have someone clean.

Cate   What's happened to your eyes?

Ian   I need you to stay, Cate. Won't be for long.

Cate   Do you know about babies?

Ian   No.

Cate   What about Matthew?

Ian   He's twenty-four.

Cate   When he was born.

Ian   They shit and cry. Hopeless.

Cate   Bleeding.

Ian   Will you touch me?

Cate   No.

Ian   So I know you're here.

Cate   You can hear me.

Ian   Won't hurt you, I promise.

Cate   (*goes to him slowly and touches the top of his head*)

Ian   Help me.

Cate   (*strokes his hair*)

Ian   Be dead soon, anyway, Cate. And it hurts. Help me to –
Help me –
Finish
It

Cate   (*withdraws her hand*)

Ian   Catie?

Cate   Got to get something for baby to eat.

Ian   Won't find anything.

Cate   May as well look.

Ian   Fucking bastards ate it all.

Cate   It'll die.

Ian   Needs its mother's milk.

Cate   Ian.

Ian   Stay. Nowhere to go, where are you going to go?
Bloody dangerous on your own, look at me.
Safer here with me.

Cate   (*considers.*
Then sits down with the baby some distance from **Ian**)

Ian   (*relaxes when he hears her sit*)

Cate   (*rocks the baby*)

Ian   Not as bad as all that, am I?

Cate   (*looks at him*)

Ian   Will you help me, Catie?

Cate   Don't know how.

Ian   Find my gun?

Cate   (*thinks. Then gets up and searches around, baby in arms. She
sees the revolver in the* **Soldier**'s *hand and stares at it for some time*)

Ian   Found it?

Cate   No.

(*She takes the revolver from the* **Soldier** *and fiddles with it.*
It springs open and she stares in at the bullets.
She removes them and closes the gun)

Ian   That it?

Cate   Yes.

Ian   Can I have it?

Cate   I don't think so.

Ian   Catie.

Cate   What?

Ian   Come on.

Cate   Don't tell me what to do.

Ian   I'm not, love. Can you keep that baby quiet.

Cate   It's not doing anything. It's hungry.

Ian   We're all bloody hungry, don't shoot myself I'll starve to death.

Cate   It's wrong to kill yourself.

Ian   No it's not.

Cate   God wouldn't like it.

Ian   There isn't one.

Cate   How do you know?

Ian   No God. No Father Christmas. No fairies. No Narnia. No fucking nothing.

Cate   Got to be something.

Ian   Why?

Cate   Doesn't make sense otherwise.

Ian   Don't be fucking stupid, doesn't make sense anyway. No reason for there to be a God just because it would be better if there was.

Cate   Thought you didn't want to die.

Ian   I can't see.

Cate   My brother's got blind friends. You can't give up.

Ian   Why not?

Cate   It's weak.

Ian   I know you want to punish me, trying to make me live.

Cate I don't.

Ian Course you fucking do, I would. There's people I'd love to suffer but they don't, they die and that's it.

Cate What if you're wrong?

Ian I'm not.

Cate But if.

Ian I've seen dead people. They're dead.
They're not somewhere else, they're dead.

Cate What about people who've seen ghosts?

Ian What about them? Imagining it.
Or making it up or wishing the person was still alive.

Cate People who've died and come back say they've seen
tunnels and lights –

Ian Can't die and come back. That's not dying, it's fainting.
When you die it's the end.

Cate I believe in God.

Ian Everything's got a scientific explanation.

Cate No.

Ian Give me my gun.

Cate What are you going to do?

Ian I won't hurt you.

Cate I know.

Ian End it. Got to, Cate, I'm ill. Just speeding it up a bit.

Cate (*thinks hard*)

Ian Please.

Cate (*gives him the gun*)

Ian (*takes the gun and puts it in his mouth.
He takes it out again*)

Don't stand behind me.

Ian (*Puts the gun back in his mouth.*
He pulls the trigger. The gun clicks, empty.
He shoots again. And again and again and again.
He takes the gun out of his mouth)

Fuck.

Cate Fate, see. You're not meant to do it. God –

Ian The cunt.

He throws the gun away in despair.

Cate (*Rocks the baby and looks down at it*)

Oh no.

Ian What.

Cate It's dead.

Ian Lucky bastard.

Cate *bursts out laughing, unnaturally, hysterically, uncontrollably.*
She laughs and laughs and laughs and laughs and laughs.

Blackout.

The sound of heavy winter rain.

Scene Five

The same.

Cate *is burying the baby under the floorboards.*

She looks around and finds two pieces of wood. She rips the lining out of
Ian's *jacket and binds the wood together in a cross which she jams*
between the boards.
She collects a few of the scattered flowers and places them under the cross.

Cate I don't know her name.

Ian Don't matter. No one's going to visit.

Cate   I was supposed to look after her.

Ian   Can bury me next to her soon. Dance on my grave.

Cate   Don't feel no pain or know nothing you shouldn't know –

Ian   Cate?

Cate   Shh.

Ian   What you doing?

Cate   Praying. Just in case.

Ian   Will you pray for me?

Cate   No.

Ian   When I'm dead, not now.

Cate   No point when you're dead.

Ian   You're praying for her.

Cate   She's baby.

Ian   So?

Cate   Innocent.

Ian   Can't you forgive me?

Cate   Don't see bad things or go bad places –

Ian   She's dead, Cate.

Cate   Or meet anyone who'll do bad things.

Ian   She won't, Cate, she's dead.

Cate   Amen.

She starts to leave.

Ian   Where you going?

Cate   I'm hungry.

Ian   Cate, it's dangerous. There's no food.

Cate   Can get some off a soldier.

Ian How?

Cate (*doesn't answer*)

Ian Don't do that.

Cate Why not?

Ian That's not you.

Cate I'm hungry.

Ian I know so am I. But.
I'd rather –
It's not –
Please, Cate.
I'm blind.

Cate I'm hungry.

She goes.

Ian Cate? Catie?
If you get some food –
Fuck.

Darkness.
Light.

Ian *masturbating.*

Ian cunt cunt cunt cunt cunt cunt cunt cunt cunt cunt cunt

Darkness.
Light.

Ian *strangling himself.*

Darkness.
Light.

Ian *shitting.*
And then trying to clean it up with newspaper.

Darkness.
Light.

Ian *laughing hysterically.*

Darkness.
Light.

Ian *having a nightmare.*

Darkness.
Light.

Ian *crying, huge bloody tears.*
He is hugging the **Soldier**'s *body for comfort.*

Darkness.
Light.

Ian *lying very still, weak with hunger.*

Darkness.
Light.

Ian *tears the cross out of the ground, rips up the boards and lifts the baby's body out.*

He eats the baby.

He puts the sheet the baby was wrapped in back in the hole.
A beat, then he climbs in after it and lies down, head poking out of the floor.

He dies with relief.

It starts to rain on him, coming through the roof.

Eventually.

Ian Shit.

Cate *enters carrying some bread, a large sausage and a bottle of gin.*
There is blood seeping from between her legs.

Cate You're sitting under a hole.

Ian I know.

Cate Get wet.

Ian Aye.

Cate Stupid bastard.

She pulls a sheet off the bed and wraps it around her.
She sits next to **Ian**'s *head.*

She eats her fill of the sausage and bread, then washes it down with gin.

Ian *listens.*

She feeds **Ian** *with the remaining food.*

She pours gin in **Ian**'s *mouth.*

She finishes feeding **Ian** *and sits apart from him, huddled for warmth.*

She drinks the gin.
She sucks her thumb.

Silence.

It rains.

Ian   Thank you.

Blackout.

Phaedra's Love

My grateful thanks to Vincent O'Connell,
Mel Kenyon and New Dramatists (New York),
without whose support I could not have written this play.

For Simon, Jo and Elana.
With love.

Phaedra's Love was first performed at the Gate Theatre, London, on 15 May 1996. The cast was as follows:

Hippolytus	Cas Harkins
Phaedra	Philippa Williams
Strophe	Catherine Cusack
Doctor/Priest/Theseus	Andrew Maud
Man 1	Giles Ward
Man 2	Paolo De Paola
Woman 1	Catherine Neal
Woman 2	Diana Penny
Policeman	Andrew Scott

Directed by Sarah Kane
Designed by Vian Curtis

Characters

Hippolytus
Doctor
Phaedra
Strophe
Priest
Theseus

Crowd including:
Man 1
Woman 1
Child
Woman 2
Man 2
Policeman 1
Policeman 2

Scene One

A royal palace.

Hippolytus *sits in a darkened room watching television.*
*He is sprawled on a sofa surrounded by expensive electronic toys, empty
crisp and sweet packets, and a scattering of used socks and underwear.*
*He is eating a hamburger, his eyes fixed on the flickering light of a
Hollywood film.*
He sniffs.
He feels a sneeze coming on and rubs his nose to stop it.
It still irritates him.
He looks around the room and picks up a sock.
He examines the sock carefully then blows his nose on it.
*He throws the sock back on the floor and continues to eat the
hamburger.*
The film becomes particularly violent.
Hippolytus *watches impassively.*
He picks up another sock, examines it and discards it.
He picks up another, examines it and decides it's fine.
*He puts his penis into the sock and masturbates until he comes without a
flicker of pleasure.*
He takes off the sock and throws it on the floor.
He begins another hamburger.

Scene Two

Doctor   He's depressed.

Phaedra   I know.

Doctor   He should change his diet. He can't live on
hamburgers and peanut butter.

Phaedra   I know.

Doctor   And wash his clothes occasionally. He smells.

Phaedra   I know. I told you this.

Doctor   What does he do all day?

Phaedra Sleep.

Doctor When he gets up.

Phaedra Watch films. And have sex.

Doctor He goes out?

Phaedra No. He phones people. They come round.
They have sex and leave.

Doctor Women?

Phaedra There's nothing gay about Hippolytus.

Doctor He should tidy his room and get some exercise.

Phaedra My mother could tell me this. I thought you
might help.

Doctor He has to help himself.

Phaedra How much do we pay you?

Doctor There's nothing clinically wrong. If he stays in bed
till four he's bound to feel low. He needs a hobby.

Phaedra He's got hobbies.

Doctor Does he have sex with you?

Phaedra I'm sorry?

Doctor Does he have sex with you?

Phaedra I'm his stepmother. We are royal.

Doctor I don't mean to be rude, but who are these people
he has sex with? Does he pay them?

Phaedra I really don't know.

Doctor He must pay them.

Phaedra He's very popular.

Doctor Why?

Phaedra He's funny.

Doctor Are you in love with him?

Phaedra   I'm married to his father.

Doctor   Does he have friends?

Phaedra   He's a prince.

Doctor   But does he have friends?

Phaedra   Why don't you ask him?

Doctor   I did. I'm asking you. Does he have friends?

Phaedra   Of course.

Doctor   Who?

Phaedra   Did you actually talk to him?

Doctor   He didn't say much.

Phaedra   I'm his friend. He talks to me.

Doctor   What about?

Phaedra   Everything.

Doctor   (*looks at her*)

Phaedra   We're very close.

Doctor   I see. And what do you think?

Phaedra   I think my son is ill. I think you should help. I think after six years training and thirty years experience the royal doctor should come up with something better than he has to lose weight.

Doctor   Who looks after things while your husband is away?

Phaedra   Me. My daughter.

Doctor   When is he coming back?

Phaedra   I've no idea.

Doctor   Are you still in love with him?

Phaedra   Of course. I haven't seen him since we married.

Doctor   You must be very lonely.

Phaedra   I have my children.

Doctor   Perhaps your son is missing his father.

Phaedra   I doubt it.

Doctor   Perhaps he's missing his real mother.

Phaedra   (*looks at him*)

Doctor   That's not a reflection on your abilities as a substitute, but there is, after all, no blood between you. I'm merely speculating.

Phaedra   Quite.

Doctor   Although he's a little old to be feeling orphaned.

Phaedra   I didn't ask you to speculate. I asked for a diagnosis. And treatment.

Doctor   He's bound to be feeling low, it's his birthday.

Phaedra   He's been like this for months.

Doctor   There's nothing wrong with him medically.

Phaedra   Medically?

Doctor   He's just very unpleasant. And therefore incurable. I'm sorry.

Phaedra   I don't know what to do.

Doctor   Get over him.

Scene Three

Strophe *is working.*
Phaedra *enters.*

Strophe   Mother.

Phaedra   Go away fuck off don't touch me don't talk to me stay with me.

Strophe   What's wrong?

Phaedra   Nothing. Nothing at all.

Strophe   I can tell.

Phaedra   Have you ever thought, thought your heart would break?

Strophe   No.

Phaedra   Wished you could cut open your chest tear it out to stop the pain?

Strophe   That would kill you.

Phaedra   This is killing me.

Strophe   No. Just feels like it.

Phaedra   A spear in my side, burning.

Strophe   Hippolytus.

Phaedra   (*screams*)

Strophe   You're in love with him.

Phaedra   (*laughs hysterically*) What are you talking about?

Strophe   Obsessed.

Phaedra   No.

Strophe   (*looks at her*)

Phaedra   Is it that obvious?

Strophe   I'm your daughter.

Phaedra   Do you think he's attractive?

Strophe   I used to.

Phaedra   What changed?

Strophe   I got to know him.

Phaedra   You don't like him?

Strophe   Not particularly.

Phaedra   You don't like Hippolytus?

Strophe   No, not really.

Phaedra   Everyone likes Hippolytus.

Strophe   I live with him.

Phaedra   It's a big house.

Strophe   He's a big man.

Phaedra   You used to spend time together.

Strophe   He wore me out.

Phaedra   You tired of Hippolytus?

Strophe   He bores me.

Phaedra   Bores you?

Strophe   Shitless.

Phaedra   Why? Everyone likes him.

Strophe   I know.

Phaedra   I know what room he's in.

Strophe   He never moves.

Phaedra   Can feel him through the walls. Sense him.
Feel his heartbeat from a mile.

Strophe   Why don't you have an affair, get your mind off
him.

Phaedra   There's a thing between us, an awesome fucking
thing, can you feel it? It burns. Meant to be. We were. Meant
to be.

Strophe   No.

Phaedra   Brought together.

Strophe   He's twenty years younger than you.

Phaedra   Want to climb inside him work him out.

Strophe   This isn't healthy.

Phaedra   He's not my son.

Strophe   You're married to his father.

Phaedra   He won't come back, too busy being useless.

Strophe   Mother. If someone were to find out.

Phaedra   Can't deny something this big.

Strophe   He's not nice to people when he's slept with them.
I've seen him.

Phaedra   Might help me get over him.

Strophe   Treats them like shit.

Phaedra   Can't switch this off. Can't crush it. Can't. Wake
up with it, burning me. Think I'll crack open I want him so
much. I talk to him. He talks to me, you know, we, we know
each other very well, he tells me things, we're very close.
About sex and how much it depresses him, and I know –

Strophe   Don't imagine you can cure him.

Phaedra   Know if it was someone who loved you,
    really loved you –

Strophe   He's poison.

Phaedra   Loved you till it burnt them –

Strophe   They do love him. Everyone loves him.
He despises them for it. You'd be no different.

Phaedra   You could feel such pleasure.

Strophe   Mother. It's me. Strophe, your daughter.
Look at me. Please. Forget this. For my sake.

Phaedra   Yours?

Strophe   You don't talk about anything else any more. You
don't work. He's all you care about, but you don't see what he
is.

Phaedra   I don't talk about him that often.

Strophe No. Most of the time you're with him. Even when you're not with him you're with him. And just occasionally, when you remember that you gave birth to me and not him, you tell me how ill he is.

Phaedra I'm worried about him.

Strophe You've said. See a doctor.

Phaedra He –

Strophe For yourself, not him.

Phaedra There's nothing wrong with me.
I don't know what to do.

Strophe Stay away from him, go and join Theseus,
fuck someone else, whatever it takes.

Phaedra I can't.

Strophe You can have any man you want.

Phaedra I want him.

Strophe Except him.

Phaedra Any man I want except the man I want.

Strophe Have you ever fucked a man more than once?

Phaedra This is different.

Strophe Mother, this family –

Phaedra Oh I know.

Strophe If anyone were to find out.

Phaedra I know, I know.

Strophe It's the excuse they're all looking for.
We'd be torn apart on the streets.

Phaedra Yes, yes, no, you're right, yes.

Strophe Think of Theseus. Why you married him.

Phaedra I can't remember.

Strophe   Then think of my father.

Phaedra   I know.

Strophe   What would he think?

Phaedra   He'd –

Strophe   Exactly. You can't do it. Can't even think of it.

Phaedra   No.

Strophe   He's a sexual disaster area.

Phaedra   Yes, I –

Strophe   No one must know. No one must know.

Phaedra   You're right, I –

Strophe   No one must know.

Phaedra   No.

Strophe   Not even Hippolytus.

Phaedra   No.

Strophe   What are you going to do?

Phaedra   Get over him.

Scene Four

Hippolytus *is watching television with the sound very low.*
He is playing with a remote control car.
It whizzes around the room.
His gaze flits between the car and the television, apparently getting pleasure from neither.
He eats from a large bag of assorted sweets on his lap.
Phaedra *enters carrying a number of wrapped presents.*
She stands for a few moments watching him.
He doesn't look at her.
Phaedra *comes further into the room.*
She puts the presents down and begins to tidy the room – she picks up

socks and underwear and looks for somewhere to put them.
There is nowhere, so she puts them back on the floor in a neat pile.
She picks up the empty crisp and sweet packets and puts them in the bin.
Hippolytus *watches the television throughout.*
Phaedra *moves to switch on a brighter light.*

Hippolytus   When was the last time you had a fuck?

Phaedra   That's not the sort of question you should ask
your stepmother.

Hippolytus   Not Theseus, then. Don't suppose he's keeping
it dry either.

Phaedra   I wish you'd call him father.

Hippolytus   Everyone wants a royal cock, I should know.

Phaedra · What are you watching?

Hippolytus   Or a royal cunt if that's your preference.

Phaedra   (*doesn't respond*)

Hippolytus   News. Another rape. Child murdered. War
somewhere. Few thousand jobs gone. But none of this matters
'cause it's a royal birthday.

Phaedra   Why don't you riot like everyone else?

Hippolytus   I don't care.

Silence.
Hippolytus *plays with his car.*

Hippolytus   Are those for me? Course they're fucking for
me.

Phaedra   People brought them to the gate. I think they'd
like to have given them to you in person. Taken photos.

Hippolytus   They're poor.

Phaedra   Yes, isn't it charming?

Hippolytus   It's revolting. (*He opens a present.*) What the
fuck am I going to do with a bagatelle? What's this? (*He shakes*

a present.) Letter-bomb. Get rid of this tat, give it to Oxfam, I don't need it.

Phaedra   It's a token of their esteem.

Hippolytus   Less than last year.

Phaedra   Have you had a good birthday?

Hippolytus   Apart from some cunt scratching my motor.

Phaedra   You don't drive.

Hippolytus   Can't now, it's scratched. Token of their contempt.

Silence.
Hippolytus *plays with his car.*

Phaedra   Who gave you that?

Hippolytus   Me. Only way of making sure I get what I want. Wrapped it up and everything.

Silence apart from the TV and car.

Phaedra   What about you?

Hippolytus   What about me? Want a sweet?

Phaedra   I –
No. Thank you.
The last time you –
What you asked me.

Hippolytus   Had a fuck.

Phaedra   Yes.

Hippolytus   Don't know. Last time I went out. When was that?

Phaedra   Months ago.

Hippolytus   Really? No. Someone came round. Fat bird. Smelt funny. And I fucked a man in the garden.

Phaedra   A man?

Hippolytus   Think so. Looked like one but you can never be sure.

(*Silence.*)

Hate me now?

Phaedra   Course not.

Silence.

Hippolytus   Where's my present, then?

Phaedra   I'm saving it.

Hippolytus   What, for next year?

Phaedra   No. I'll give it to you later.

Hippolytus   When?

Phaedra   Soon.

Hippolytus   Why not now?

Phaedra   Soon. I promise. Soon.

They look at each other in silence.
Hippolytus *looks away.*
He sniffs.
He picks up a sock and examines it.
He smells it.

Phaedra   That's disgusting.

Hippolytus   What is?

Phaedra   Blowing your nose on your sock.

Hippolytus   Only after I've checked I haven't cleaned my cum up with it first.
And I do have them washed.
Before I wear them.

(*Silence.*
He crashes the car into the wall.)

What is wrong with you?

Phaedra   What do you mean?

Hippolytus   I was born into this shit, you married it. Was he a great shag? Fucking must have been. Every man in the country is sniffing round your cunt and you pick Theseus, man of the people, what a wanker.

Phaedra   You only ever talk to me about sex.

Hippolytus   It's my main interest.

Phaedra   I thought you hated it.

Hippolytus   I hate people.

Phaedra   They don't hate you.

Hippolytus   No. They buy me bagatelles.

Phaedra   I meant –

Hippolytus   I know what you meant.
You're right. Women find me much more
attractive since I've become fat.
They think I must have a secret.

(*He blows his nose on the sock and discards it.*)

I'm fat. I'm disgusting. I'm miserable.
But I get lots of sex. Therefore . . . ?

(*He looks at* **Phaedra**. *She doesn't respond.*)

Come on, Mother, work it out.

Phaedra   Don't call me that.

Hippolytus   Therefore. I must be very good at it. Yes?

Phaedra   (*doesn't respond*)

Hippolytus   Why shouldn't I call you mother, Mother? I thought that's what was required. One big happy family. The only popular royals ever. Or does it make you feel old?

Phaedra   (*doesn't respond*)

Hippolytus   Hate me now?

Phaedra Why do you want me to hate you?

Hippolytus I don't. But you will. In the end.

Phaedra Never.

Hippolytus They all do.

Phaedra Not me.

They stare at each other.
Hippolytus *looks away.*

Hippolytus Why don't you go and talk to Strophe, she's
your child, I'm not. Why all this concern for me?

Phaedra I love you.

Silence.

Hippolytus Why?

Phaedra You're difficult. Moody, cynical, bitter, fat,
decadent, spoilt. You stay in bed all day then watch TV all
night, you crash around this house with sleep in your eyes and
not a thought for anyone. You're in pain. I adore you.

Hippolytus Not very logical.

Phaedra Love isn't.

Hippolytus *and* **Phaedra** *look at each other in silence.*
He turns back to the television and car.

Phaedra Have you ever thought about having sex with
me?

Hippolytus I think about having sex with everyone.

Phaedra Would it make you happy?

Hippolytus That's not the word exactly.

Phaedra No, but –
Would you enjoy it?

Hippolytus No. I never do.

Phaedra Then why do it?

Hippolytus   Life's too long.

Phaedra   I think you'd enjoy it. With me.

Hippolytus   Some people do, I suppose. Enjoy that stuff.
Have a life.

Phaedra   You've got a life.

Hippolytus   No. Filling up time. Waiting.

Phaedra   For what?

Hippolytus   Don't know. Something to happen.

Phaedra   This is happening.

Hippolytus   Never does.

Phaedra   Now.

Hippolytus   Till then. Fill it up with tat.
Bric-a-brac, bits and bobs, getting by,
Christ Almighty wept.

Phaedra   Fill it up with me.

Hippolytus   Some people have it. They're not marking
time, they're living. Happy. With a lover.
Hate them.

Phaedra   Why?

Hippolytus   Getting dark thank Christ day's nearly over.

A long silence.

If we fuck we'll never talk again.

Phaedra   I'm not like that.

Hippolytus   I am.

Phaedra   I'm not.

Hippolytus   Course you are.

They stare at each other.

Phaedra   I'm in love with you.

Hippolytus   Why?

Phaedra   You thrill me.

Silence.

>   Would you like your present now?

Hippolytus   (*looks at her. Then turns back to the TV*)

Silence.

Phaedra   I don't know what to do.

Hippolytus   Go away. It's obviously the only thing to do.

They both stare at the television.
Eventually, **Phaedra** *moves over to* **Hippolytus**.
He doesn't look at her.
She undoes his trousers and performs oral sex on him.
He watches the screen throughout and eats his sweets.
As he is about to come he makes a sound.
Phaedra *begins to move her head away – he holds it down and comes in*
her mouth without taking his eyes off the television.
He releases her head.
Phaedra *sits up and looks at the television.*
A long silence, broken only by the rustling of **Hippolytus**' *sweet bag.*
Phaedra *cries.*

Hippolytus   There. Mystery over.

Silence.

Phaedra   Will you get jealous?

Hippolytus   Of what?

Phaedra   When your father comes back.

Hippolytus   What's it got to do with me?

Phaedra   I've never been unfaithful before.

Hippolytus   That much was obvious.

Phaedra   I'm sorry.

Hippolytus   I've had worse.

Phaedra   I did it because I'm in love with you.

Hippolytus   Don't be. I don't like it.

Phaedra   I want this to happen again.

Hippolytus   No you don't.

Phaedra   I do.

Hippolytus   What for?

Phaedra   Pleasure?

Hippolytus   You enjoyed that?

Phaedra   I want to be with you.

Hippolytus   But did you enjoy it?

Silence.

No. You hate it as much as me if only you'd
admit it.

Phaedra   I wanted to see your face when you came.

Hippolytus   Why?

Phaedra   I'd like to see you lose yourself.

Hippolytus   It's not a pleasant sight.

Phaedra   Why, what do you look like?

Hippolytus   Every other stupid fucker.

Phaedra   I love you.

Hippolytus   No.

Phaedra   So much.

Hippolytus   Don't even know me.

Phaedra   I want you to make me come.

Hippolytus   I'm not used to post-coital chats.
There's never anything to say.

Phaedra   I want you –

Hippolytus   This isn't about me.

Phaedra   I do.

Hippolytus   Fuck someone else imagine it's me. Shouldn't be difficult, everyone looks the same when they come.

Phaedra   Not when they burn you.

Hippolytus   No one burns me.

Phaedra   What about that woman?

Silence.
Hippolytus *looks at her.*

Hippolytus   What?

Phaedra   Lena, weren't you –

Hippolytus *grabs* **Phaedra** *by the throat.*

Hippolytus   Don't ever mention her again.
Don't say her name to me, don't refer to her,
don't even think about her, understand?
Understand?

Phaedra   (*nods*)

Hippolytus   No one burns me, no one fucking touches me.
So don't try.

He releases her.
Silence.

Phaedra   Why do you have sex if you hate it so much?

Hippolytus   I'm bored.

Phaedra   I thought you were supposed to be good at it.
Is everyone this disappointed?

Hippolytus   Not when I try.

Phaedra   When do you try?

Hippolytus   Don't any more.

Phaedra   Why not?

Hippolytus   It's boring.

Phaedra   You're just like your father.

Hippolytus   That's what your daughter said.

A beat, then **Phaedra** *slaps him around the face as hard as she can.*

Hippolytus   She's less passionate but more practiced.
I go for technique every time.

Phaedra   Did you make her come?

Hippolytus   Yes.

Phaedra   (*opens her mouth to speak. She can't*)

Hippolytus   It's dead now. Face it. Can't happen again.

Phaedra   Why not?

Hippolytus   Wouldn't be about me. Never was.

Phaedra   You can't stop me loving you.

Hippolytus   Can.

Phaedra   No. You're alive.

Hippolytus   Wake up.

Phaedra   You burn me.

Hippolytus   Now you've had me, fuck someone else.

Silence.

Phaedra   Will I see you again?

Hippolytus   You know where I am.

Silence.

Do I get my present now?

Phaedra   (*opens her mouth but is momentarily lost for words.
Then*)
You're a heartless bastard.

Hippolytus   Exactly.

Phaedra *begins to leave.*

Hippolytus   Phaedra.

Phaedra   (*looks at him*)

Hippolytus   See a doctor. I've got gonorrhoea.

Phaedra   (*opens her mouth. No sound comes out*)

Hippolytus   Hate me now?

Phaedra   (*tries to speak. A long silence. Eventually*)
      No.
      Why do you hate me?

Hippolytus   Because you hate yourself.

Phaedra *leaves.*

Scene Five

Hippolytus *is standing in front of a mirror with his tongue out.*
Strophe *enters.*

Strophe   Hide.

Hippolytus   Green tongue.

Strophe   Hide, idiot.

Hippolytus *turns to her and shows her his tongue.*

Hippolytus   Fucking moss. Inch of pleurococcus on my
tongue. Looks like the top of a wall.

Strophe   Hippolytus.

Hippolytus   Showed it to a bloke in the bogs,
      still wanted to shag me.

Strophe   Have you looked out the window?

Hippolytus   Major halitosis.

Strophe   Look.

Hippolytus   Haven't seen you for ages, how are you?

Strophe   Burning.

Hippolytus   You'd never know we live in the same house.

Strophe   For fuck's sake, hide.

Hippolytus   Why, what have I done?

Strophe   My mother's accusing you of rape.

Hippolytus   She is? How exciting.

Strophe   This isn't a joke.

Hippolytus   I'm sure.

Strophe   Did you do it?

Hippolytus   What?

Strophe   Did you rape her?

Hippolytus   I don't know. What does that mean?

Strophe   Did you have sex with her?

Hippolytus   Ah. Got you.
Does it matter?

Strophe   Does it *matter*?

Hippolytus   Does it matter.

Strophe   Yes.

Hippolytus   Why?

Strophe   *Why?*

Hippolytus   Yes, why, I do wish you wouldn't repeat
everything I say, why?

Strophe   She's my mother.

Hippolytus   So?

Strophe   My mother says she was raped.
She says you raped her.
I want to know if you had sex with my mother.

Hippolytus   Because she's your mother or because of what people will say?

Strophe   Because she's my mother.

Hippolytus   Because you still want me or because you want to know if she was better than you?

Strophe   Because she's my mother.

Hippolytus   Because she's your mother.

Strophe   Did you have sex with her?

Hippolytus   I don't think so.

Strophe   Was there any sexual contact between you and my mother?

Hippolytus   Sexual contact?

Strophe   You know exactly what I mean.

Hippolytus   Don't get stroppy, Strophe.

Strophe   Did she want to do it?

Hippolytus   You should have been a lawyer.

Strophe   Did you make her?

Hippolytus   You're wasted as a pseudo-princess.

Strophe   Did you force her?

Hippolytus   Did I force you?

Strophe   There aren't words for what you did to me.

Hippolytus   Then perhaps rape is the best she can do.
                    Me. A rapist. Things are looking up.

Strophe   Hippolytus.

Hippolytus   At the very least it's not boring.

Strophe   You'll be lynched for this.

Hippolytus   Do you think?

Strophe   If you did it I'll help them.

Hippolytus   Of course. Not my sister after all. One of my victims.

Strophe   If you didn't I'll stand by you.

Hippolytus   A rapist?

Strophe   Burn with you.

Hippolytus   Why?

Strophe   Sake of the family.

Hippolytus   Ah.

Strophe   You're my brother.

Hippolytus   No I'm not.

Strophe   To me.

Hippolytus   Strange. The one person in this family who has no claim to its history is the most sickeningly loyal. Poor relation who wants to be what she never will.

Strophe   I'll die for this family.

Hippolytus   Yes. You probably will.
I told her about us.

Strophe   You what?

Hippolytus   Yes. And I mentioned that you'd had her husband.

Strophe   No.

Hippolytus   I didn't say you fucked him on their wedding night, but since he left the day after –

Strophe   Mother.

Hippolytus   A rapist. Better than a fat boy who fucks.

Strophe   You're smiling.

Hippolytus   I am.

Strophe   You're a heartless bastard, you know that?

Hippolytus   It's been said.

Strophe   This is your fault.

Hippolytus   Of course.

Strophe   She was my mother, Hippolytus, my mother.
What did you do to her?

Hippolytus   (*looks at her*)

Strophe   She's dead you fucking bastard.

Hippolytus   Don't be stupid.

Strophe   Yes.
What did you do to her, what did you fucking do?

Strophe *batters him about the head.*
Hippolytus *catches her arms and holds her so she can't hit him.*
Strophe *sobs, then breaks down and cries, then wails uncontrollably.*

Strophe   What have I done? What have I done?

Hippolytus' *hold turns into an embrace.*

Hippolytus   Wasn't you, Strophe, you're not to blame.

Strophe   Never even told her I loved her.

Hippolytus   She knew.

Strophe   No.

Hippolytus   She was your mother.

Strophe   She –

Hippolytus   She knew, she knew, she loved you.
Nothing to blame yourself for.

Strophe   You told her about us.

Hippolytus   Then blame me.

Strophe   You told her about Theseus.

Hippolytus   Yes. Blame me.

Strophe   You –

Hippolytus   Me. Blame me.

A long silence.
Hippolytus *and* **Strophe** *hold each other.*

Hippolytus   What happened?

Strophe   Hung.

       (*Silence.*)

       Note saying you'd raped her.

A long silence.

Hippolytus   She shouldn't have taken it so seriously.

Strophe   She loved you.

Hippolytus   (*looks at her*) Did she?

Strophe   Tell me you didn't rape her.

Hippolytus   Love me?

Strophe   Tell me you didn't do it.

Hippolytus   She says I did and she's dead. Believe her.
Easier all round.

Strophe   What is wrong with you?

Hippolytus   This is her present to me.

Strophe   What?

Hippolytus   Not many people get a chance like this.
This isn't tat. This isn't bric-a-brac.

Strophe   Deny it. There's a riot.

Hippolytus   Life at last.

Strophe   Burning down the palace. You have to deny it.

Hippolytus   Are you insane? She died doing this for me.
I'm doomed.

Strophe   Deny it.

Hippolytus   Absolutely fucking doomed.

Strophe For me. Deny it.

Hippolytus No.

Strophe You're not a rapist. I can't believe that.

Hippolytus Me neither.

Strophe Please.

Hippolytus Fucked. Finished.

Strophe I'll help you hide.

Hippolytus She really did love me.

Strophe You didn't do it.

Hippolytus Bless her.

Strophe Did you.

Hippolytus No. I didn't.

He begins to leave.

Strophe Where are you going?

Hippolytus I'm turning myself in.

He leaves.
Strophe *sits alone for a few moments thinking.*
She gets up and follows him.

Scene Six

A prison cell.

Hippolytus *sits alone.*
A **Priest** *enters.*

Priest My son.

Hippolytus Bit of a come down. Always suspected the world didn't smell of fresh paint and flowers.

Priest I may be able to help you.

Hippolytus   Smells of piss and human sweat. Most unpleasant.

Priest   Son.

Hippolytus   You're not my father. He won't be visiting.

Priest   Is there anything you need?

Hippolytus   Got a single cell.

Priest   I can help you.

Hippolytus   Don't need tat.

Priest   Spiritually.

Hippolytus   Beyond that.

Priest   No one is beyond redemption.

Hippolytus   Nothing to confess.

Priest   Your sister told us.

Hippolytus   Us?

Priest   She explained the situation to me.

Hippolytus   She's not my sister.
Admit, yes. Confess, no. I admit it. The rape.
I did it.

Priest   Do you feel remorse?

Hippolytus   Will you be giving evidence?

Priest   That depends.

Hippolytus   No. No remorse. Joy, in fact.

Priest   At your mother's death?

Hippolytus   Suicide, not death. She wasn't my mother.

Priest   You feel joy at your stepmother's suicide?

Hippolytus   No. She was human.

Priest   So where do you find your joy?

Hippolytus Within.

Priest I find that hard to believe.

Hippolytus Course you do. You think life has no meaning unless we have another person in it to torture us.

Priest I have no one to torture me.

Hippolytus You have the worst lover of all. Not only does he think he's perfect, he is. I'm satisfied to be alone.

Priest Self-satisfaction is a contradiction in terms.

Hippolytus I can rely on me. I never let me down.

Priest True satisfaction comes from love.

Hippolytus What when love dies? Alarm clock rings it's time to wake up, what then?

Priest Love never dies. It evolves.

Hippolytus You're dangerous.

Priest Into respect. Consideration.
Have you considered your family?

Hippolytus What about it?

Priest It's not an ordinary family.

Hippolytus No. None of us are related to each other.

Priest Royalty is chosen. Because you are more privileged than most you are also more culpable. God –

Hippolytus There is no God. There is. No God.

Priest Perhaps you'll find there is. And what will you do then? There's no repentance in the next life, only in this one.

Hippolytus What do you suggest, a last-minute conversion just in case? Die as if there is a God, knowing that there isn't? No. If there is a God, I'd like to look him in the face knowing I'd died as I'd lived. In conscious sin.

Priest Hippolytus.

Hippolytus   I'm sure God would be intelligent enough to see through any eleventh-hour confession of mine.

Priest   Do you know what the unforgivable sin is?

Hippolytus   Of course.

Priest   You are in danger of committing it. It's not just your soul at stake, it's the future of your family –

Hippolytus   Ah.

Priest   Your country.

Hippolytus   Why do I always forget this?

Priest   Your sexual indiscretions are of no interest to anyone. But the stability of the nation's morals is. You are a guardian of those morals. You will answer to God for the collapse of the country you and your family lead.

Hippolytus   I'm not responsible.

Priest   Then deny the rape. And confess that sin. Now.

Hippolytus   Before I've committed it?

Priest   Too late after.

Hippolytus   Yes. The nature of the sin precludes confession. I couldn't confess if I wanted to. I don't want to. That's the sin. Correct?

Priest   It's not too late.

Hippolytus   Correct.

Priest   God is merciful. He chose you.

Hippolytus   Bad choice.

Priest   Pray with me. Save yourself. And your country. Don't commit that sin.

Hippolytus   What bothers you more, the destruction of my soul or the end of my family? I'm not in danger of committing the unforgivable sin. I already have.

Priest   Don't say it.

Hippolytus   Fuck God. Fuck the monarchy.

Priest   Lord, look down on this man you chose, forgive his sin which comes from the intelligence you blessed him with.

Hippolytus   I can't sin against a God I don't believe in.

Priest   No.

Hippolytus   A non-existent God can't forgive.

Priest   No. You must forgive yourself.

Hippolytus   I've lived by honesty let me die by it.

Priest   If truth is your absolute you will die.
If life is your absolute –

Hippolytus   I've chosen my path. I'm fucking doomed.

Priest   No.

Hippolytus   Let me die.

Priest   No. Forgive yourself.

Hippolytus   (*thinks hard*)
I can't.

Priest   Why not?

Hippolytus   Do you believe in God?

Priest   (*looks at him*)

Hippolytus   I know what I am. And always will be. But you. You sin knowing you'll confess. Then you're forgiven. And then you start all over again. How do you dare mock a God so powerful? Unless you don't really believe.

Priest   This is your confession, not mine.

Hippolytus   Then why are you on your knees? God certainly is merciful. If I were him I'd despise you. I'd wipe you off the face of the earth for your dishonesty.

Priest   You're not God.

Hippolytus   No. A prince. God on earth. But not God.
Fortunate for all concerned. I'd not allow you to sin knowing
you'd confess and get away with it.

Priest   Heaven would be empty.

Hippolytus   A kingdom of honest men, honestly sinning.
And death for those who try to cover their arse.

Priest   What do you think forgiveness is?

Hippolytus   It may be enough for you, but I have no
intention of covering my arse. I killed a woman and I will be
punished for it by hypocrites who I shall take down with me.
May we burn in hell. God may be all powerful, but there's one
thing he can't do.

Priest   There is a kind of purity in you.

Hippolytus   He can't make me good.

Priest   No.

Hippolytus   Last line of defence for the honest man.
Free will is what distinguishes us from the
animals.

(*He undoes his trousers.*)

And I have no intention of behaving like a
fucking animal.

Priest   (*performs oral sex on* **Hippolytus**)

Hippolytus   Leave that to you.

(*He comes.*
He rests his hand on top of the **Priest**'s *head.*)

Go.
Confess.
Before you burn.

Scene Seven

Phaedra's *body lies on a funeral pyre, covered.*
Theseus *enters.*
He approaches the pyre.
He lifts the cover and looks at **Phaedra**'s *face.*
He lets the cover drop.
He kneels by **Phaedra**'s *body.*
He tears at his clothes, then skin, then hair, more and more frantically until he is exhausted.
But he does not cry.
He stands and lights the funeral pyre – **Phaedra** *goes up in flames.*

Theseus   I'll kill him.

Scene Eight

Outside the court.

A crowd of **Men**, **Women** *and* **Children** *has gathered around a fire, including* **Theseus** *and* **Strophe**, *both disguised.*

Theseus   Come far?

Man 1   Newcastle.

Woman 1   Brought the kids.

Child   And a picnic.

Man 1   String him up, they should.

Woman 2   The bastard.

Man 1   Whole fucking pack of them.

Woman 1   Set an example.

Man 1   What do they take us for?

Woman 1   Parasites.

Man 2   We pay the raping bastard.

Man 1   No more.

Man 2   They're nothing special.

Woman 1   Raped his own mother.

Woman 2   The bastard.

Man 2   She was the only one had anything going for her.

Theseus   He'll walk.

Man 2   I'll be waiting at the fucking gate.

Man 1   Won't be the only one.

Woman 1   He's admitted it.

Strophe   That means nothing.

Woman 2   The bastard.

Theseus   Might go in his favour. Sorry your honour, reading my bible every day, never do it again, case dismissed. Not going to lock a prince up, are they? Whatever he's done.

Man 2   That's right.

Man 1   No justice.

Theseus   Member of the royal family. Crown against the crown? They're not stupid.

Man 1   Pig-shit thick, the lot of them.

Man 2   She was all right.

Man 1   She's dead.

Theseus   You don't hang on to the crown for centuries without something between your ears.

Man 2   That's right.

Theseus   Show trial. Him in the dock, sacrifice the reputation of a minor prince, expel him from the family.

Man 2   Exactly, exactly.

Theseus   Say they've rid themselves of the corrupting element. But the monarchy remains intact.

Man 1   What shall we do?

Man 2   Justice for all.

Woman 1   He must die.

Man 2   Has to die.

Man 1   For our sake.

Man 2   And hers.

Woman 1   Don't deserve to live. I've got kids.

Man 1   We've all got kids.

Woman 1   You got kids?

Theseus   Not any more.

Woman 2   Poor bastard.

Man 2   Knows what we're talking about then, don't he.

Man 1   Scum should die.

Woman 1   Here he comes.

Woman 2   The bastard.

As **Hippolytus** *is taken past, the crowd scream abuse and hurl rocks.*

Woman 2   Bastard!

Man 1   Die, scum!

Woman 1   Rot in hell, bastard!

Man 2   Royal raping bastard!

Hippolytus *breaks free from the* **Policemen** *holding him and hurls himself into the crowd.*
He falls into the arms of **Theseus**.

Man 1   Kill him. Kill the royal slag.

Hippolytus *looks into* **Theseus'** *face.*

Hippolytus   You.

Theseus *hesitates, then kisses him full on the lips and pushes him into the arms of* **Man 2**.

Theseus   Kill him.

Man 2 *holds* **Hippolytus**.
Man 1 *takes a tie from around a child's neck and puts it around* **Hippolytus'** *throat.*
He strangles **Hippolytus**, *who is kicked by the* **Women** *as he chokes into semi-consciousness.*
Woman 2 *produces a knife.*

Strophe   No! No! Don't hurt him, don't kill him!

Man 2   Listen to her.

Man 1   Defending an in-bred.

Woman 1   What sort of a woman are you?

Theseus   Defending a rapist.

Theseus *pulls* **Strophe** *away from* **Woman 2** *who she is attacking.*
He rapes her.
The crowd watch and cheer.
When **Theseus** *has finished he cuts her throat.*

Strophe   Theseus.
Hippolytus.
Innocent.
Mother.
Oh, Mother.

She dies.
Man 1 *pulls down* **Hippolytus'** *trousers.*
Woman 2 *cuts off his genitals.*
They are thrown onto the fire.
The children cheer.
A child pulls them out of the fire and throws them at another child, who screams and runs away.
Much laughter.
Someone retrieves them and they are thrown to a dog.
Theseus *takes the knife.*

He cuts **Hippolytus** *from groin to chest.*
Hippolytus' *bowels are torn out and thrown onto the fire.*
He is kicked and stoned and spat on.
Hippolytus *looks at the body of* **Strophe**.

Hippolytus   Strophe.

Theseus   Strophe.

Theseus *looks closely at the woman he has raped and murdered.*
He recognises her with horror.
When **Hippolytus** *is completely motionless, the police who have been watching wade into the crowd, hitting them randomly.*
The crowd disperses with the exception of **Theseus**.
Two **Policemen** *stand looking down at* **Hippolytus**.

Policeman 1   Poor bastard.

Policeman 2   You joking?

(*He kicks* **Hippolytus** *hard.*)

I've got two daughters.

Policeman 1   Should move him.

Policeman 2   Let him rot.

Policeman 2 *spits on* **Hippolytus**.
They leave.
Hippolytus *is motionless.*
Theseus *is sitting by* **Strophe**'s *body.*

Theseus   Hippolytus.
Son.
I never liked you.
(*To* **Strophe**.)
I'm sorry.
Didn't know it was you.
God forgive me I didn't know.
If I'd known it was you I'd never have –
(*To* **Hippolytus**.)
You hear me, I didn't know.

Theseus *cuts his own throat and bleeds to death.*

The three bodies lie completely still.
Eventually, **Hippolytus** *opens his eyes and looks at the sky.*

Hippolytus   Vultures.

(*He manages a smile.*)

If there could have been more moments like this.

(*He dies.*)

A vulture descends and begins to eat his body.

Methuen Modern Plays

include work by

Jean Anouilh
John Arden
Margaretta D'Arcy
Peter Barnes
Sebastian Barry
Brendan Behan
Edward Bond
Bertolt Brecht
Howard Brenton
Simon Burke
Jim Cartwright
Caryl Churchill
Noël Coward
Sarah Daniels
Nick Dear
Shelagh Delaney
David Edgar
Dario Fo
Michael Frayn
John Godber
Paul Godfrey
John Guare
Peter Handke
Jonathan Harvey
Iain Heggie
Declan Hughes
Terry Johnson
Barrie Keeffe
Stephen Lowe
Doug Lucie

John McGrath
David Mamet
Patrick Marber
Arthur Miller
Mtwa, Ngema & Simon
Tom Murphy
Phyllis Nagy
Peter Nichols
Joseph O'Connor
Joe Orton
Louise Page
Joe Penhall
Luigi Pirandello
Stephen Poliakoff
Franca Rame
Philip Ridley
Reginald Rose
David Rudkin
Willy Russell
Jean-Paul Sartre
Sam Shepard
Wole Soyinka
C. P. Taylor
Theatre de Complicite
Theatre Workshop
Sue Townsend
Judy Upton
Timberlake Wertenbaker
Victoria Wood

Methuen World Classics

Aeschylus (two volumes)
Jean Anouilh
John Arden (two volumes)
Arden & D'Arcy
Aristophanes (two volumes)
Aristophanes & Menander
Brendan Behan
Aphra Behn
Edward Bond (four volumes)
Bertolt Brecht
   (five volumes)
Büchner
Bulgakov
Calderón
Anton Chekhov
Noël Coward (five volumes)
Sarah Daniels (two volumes)
Eduardo De Filippo
David Edgar (three volumes)
Euripides (three volumes)
Dario Fo (two volumes)
Michael Frayn (two volumes)
Max Frisch
Gorky
Harley Granville Barker
   (two volumes)
Henrik Ibsen (six volumes)
Terry Johnson
Lorca (three volumes)

Marivaux
Mustapha Matura
David Mercer (two volumes)
Arthur Miller
   (five volumes)
Anthony Minghella
Molière
Tom Murphy
   (three volumes)
Musset
Peter Nichols (two volumes)
Clifford Odets
Joe Orton
Louise Page
A. W. Pinero
Luigi Pirandello
Stephen Poliakoff
   (two volumes)
Terence Rattigan
Ntozake Shange
Sophocles (two volumes)
Wole Soyinka
David Storey (two volumes)
August Strindberg
   (three volumes)
J. M. Synge
Ramón del Valle-Inclán
Frank Wedekind
Oscar Wilde

Methuen Student Editions

John Arden	*Serjeant Musgrave's Dance*
Alan Ayckbourn	*Confusions*
Aphra Behn	*The Rover*
Edward Bond	*Lear*
Bertolt Brecht	*The Caucasian Chalk Circle*
	Life of Galileo
	Mother Courage and her Childr
Anton Chekhov	*The Cherry Orchard*
Caryl Churchill	*Top Girls*
Shelagh Delaney	*A Taste of Honey*
John Galsworthy	*Strife*
Robert Holman	*Across Oka*
Henrik Ibsen	*A Doll's House*
Charlotte Keatley	*My Mother Said I Never Shoulc*
John Marston	*The Malcontent*
Willy Russell	*Blood Brothers*
August Strindberg	*The Father*
J. M. Synge	*The Playboy of the Western Wo*
Oscar Wilde	*The Importance of Being Earne*
Tennessee Williams	*A Streetcar Named Desire*
Timberlake Wertenbaker	*Our Country's Good*